Eight Days Gone

Linda McReynolds

Illustrated by Ryan O'Rourke

⌂ Charlesbridge

Hundreds gather.
Hot July.
Spaceship ready—
set to fly.

620046662

Launchpad countdown.
Smoke and flame.
Rumbling. Blasting.
Seizing fame.

Rocket orbits.

Engines fire.

Toward the moon.

Soaring higher.

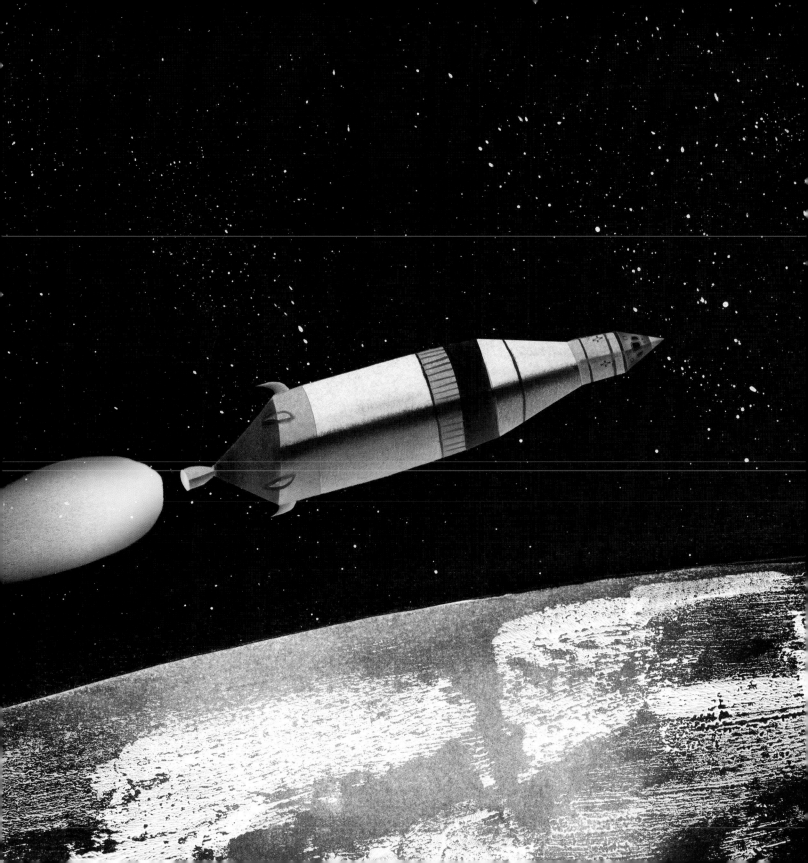

Shrinking planet.
Streaming fast.
Starry darkness.
Sprawling, vast.

Fasten helmets,
gloves, and boots.
Backpacks, air tanks,
bulky suits.

Spacecraft readied.
System checks.
Lunar module
disconnects.

Michael Collins
stays with ship.
Waits, observing,
tracking trip.

Nation watching,
bated breath.
Eagle landing—
life or death.

Armstrong makes his
one small step.
Giant leap from
years of prep.

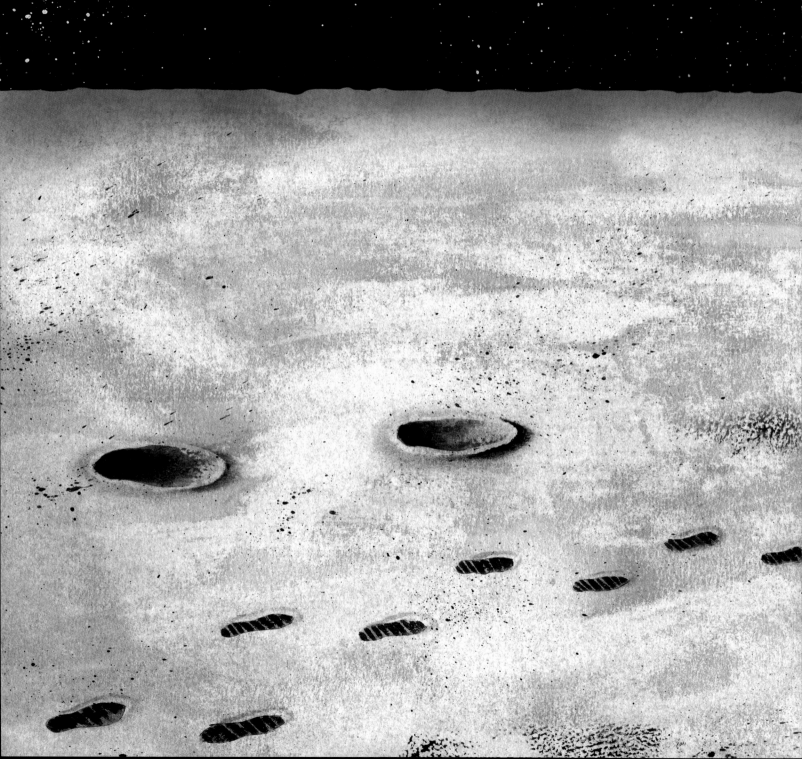

Edwin Aldrin
hops around.
Boot prints left on
ashen ground.

Desolation.
Silent. Dark.
Tranquil sea.
Barren. Stark.

Haul equipment.
Careful test.
Exploration.
Lunar quest.

Snapping pictures,
planting flag.
Soil samples,
rocks in bag.

Eagle docking—
mission ends.
Journey home to
family, friends.

Swiftly speeding.
Earth ahead.
Ship arriving.
News is spread.

Ocean splashdown.
Heroes seen.
Helicopter.
Quarantine.

Brave explorers—
safe return.
Data gathered.
Much to learn.

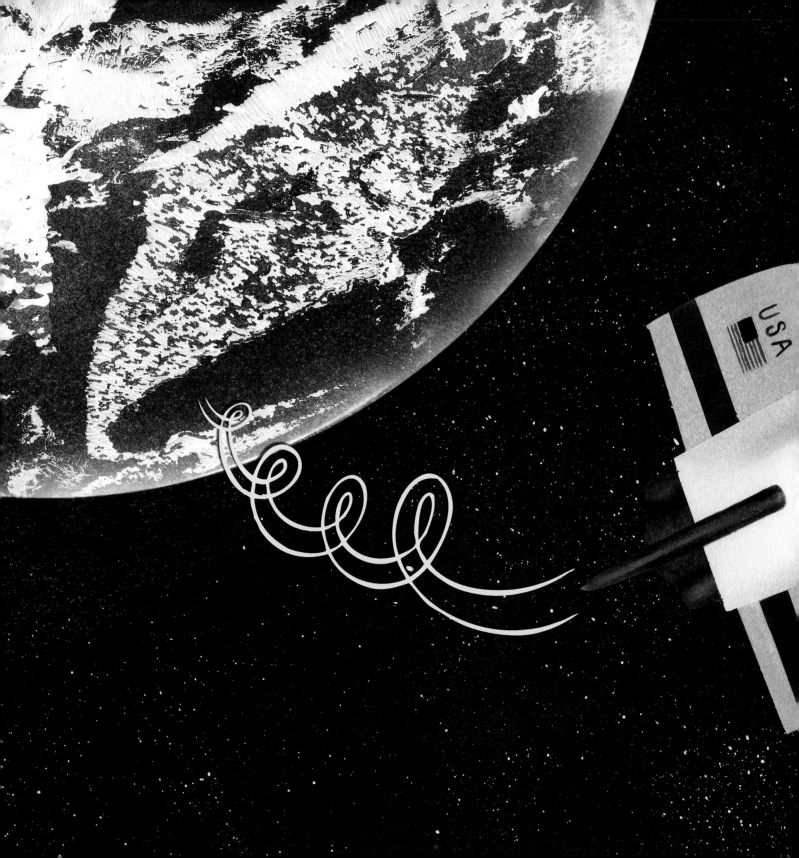

Lunar mission
reached new heights.
Paved the way
for future flights.

Author's Note

On July 16, 1969, the Apollo 11 mission to the moon began with the launch of a Saturn V rocket from Kennedy Space Center in Florida. After being thrust through space, the command module, *Columbia*, and the lunar module, *Eagle*, separated from the rocket and headed for the moon. On board were three astronauts: Neil Armstrong, Edwin "Buzz" Aldrin, and Michael Collins.

On July 20, *Eagle* detached from *Columbia* and made its descent to the lunar surface. Collins remained aboard *Columbia*, orbiting the moon, while the other two astronauts landed *Eagle* on an area of the moon called the Sea of Tranquility.

Armstrong and Aldrin performed scientific tests and collected samples of soil and rock. After two and a half hours, the astronauts planted an American flag as a reminder of their visit and left the lunar surface.

Eagle rejoined *Columbia*, and the crew began its journey home. Once *Columbia* reentered the Earth's atmosphere, parachutes opened and safely lowered the module into the Pacific Ocean. The crew was picked up by helicopter and taken to the *USS Hornet*, a nearby recovery ship.

Because traveling to the moon had never been done before, scientists were uncertain whether it would have any negative effects on humans. The astronauts were put in quarantine until it was determined that they were not sick from their journey. While in quarantine, the heroes were visited by President Richard M. Nixon.

Although the entire mission lasted only eight days, its historic nature makes it one of the most famous missions of the space program. It also fulfilled President John F. Kennedy's dream of sending a man to the moon and bringing him safely back to Earth before the end of the 1960s.

This photo shows the lunar module ascent prior to its docking with the command module. Photo date: July 21, 1969. Photo source: NASA.

Bibliography

Books

Charleston, Gordon. *Armstrong Lands on the Moon*. New York: Macmillan Publishing Company, 1994.

Stein, R. Conrad. *Apollo 11*. Chicago: Children's Press, 1992.

Websites

Kidport Reference Library: The Moon Landing
http://www.kidport.com/reflib/science/moonlanding/moonlanding.htm

This is an online reference library designed to be fun and easy for children to use. In addition to information about space travel, there is plenty to discover about other areas of science, social studies, and language arts.

NASA—Kennedy Space Center Home Page
http://www.nasa.gov/centers/kennedy/home/index.html

The official website of the National Aeronautics and Space Administration (NASA) contains a wealth of information on all aspects of space exploration, including the Apollo 11 mission.

We Choose the Moon: Pre-launch
http://wechoosethemoon.org/

Created by the John F. Kennedy Library and Museum, this interactive site allows kids to see animated scenes of each stage of the Apollo 11 mission, as well as archival photos, videos, and audio clips from the lunar mission. At the end of the mission, kids can download a certificate that states they have "landed on the moon and returned safely to Earth."

To Mom and Dad, who have encouraged and
supported my dream of becoming an author
ever since I learned to write

—L. M.

For my parents

—R. O.

Text copyright © 2012 by Linda McReynolds
Illustrations copyright © 2012 by Ryan O'Rourke
All rights reserved, including the right of reproduction in
whole or in part in any form. Charlesbridge and colophon are
registered trademarks of Charlesbridge Publishing, Inc.

Published by Charlesbridge
85 Main Street
Watertown, MA 02472
(617) 926-0329
www.charlesbridge.com

Illustrations done in oils on illustration board
Display type and text type set in Changing and Candy Square
Color separations by KHL Chroma Graphics, Singapore
Printed and bound February 2012 by Imago in Singapore
Production supervision by Brian G. Walker
Designed by Diane M. Earley

Library of Congress Cataloging-in-Publication Data
McReynolds, Linda.
    Eight days gone / Linda McReynolds ; illustrated by Ryan
O'Rourke.
      p. cm.
    ISBN 978-1-58089-364-0 (reinforced for library use)
    ISBN 978-1-58089-365-7 (softcover)
1. Project Apollo (U.S.)—Juvenile literature. 2. Space flight
to the moon—Juvenile literature. 3. Apollo 11 (Spacecraft)—
Juvenile literature. I. O'Rourke, Ryan, ill. II. Title.
TL789.8.U6M55536 2012
629.45'4—dc23   2011025776

Printed in Singapore
(hc) 10 9 8 7 6 5 4 3 2 1
(sc) 10 9 8 7 6 5 4 3 2 1